DON'T COOK FISH IN THE COMPANY MICROWAVE

How to Advance Your Career
and Improve Your Life

by
Tim Shortridge

Don't Cook Fish in the Company Microwave:

How to Advance Your Career and Improve Your Life

Copyright © 2015 Tim Shortridge

All rights reserved.
This includes the right to reproduce any portion of this book in any form without prior written permission of the author.
Copyright © First Edition (August, 2008)

*For our daughter, Melanie,
may your success exceed my own.*

*And for our son, Richard,
may you rest in peace.*

We love you both past anything...

Also by
Tim Shortridge:

No Place To Run

Understand Accounting Without Falling Asleep

Out of Plumb

Sealing Fate

Table of Contents

FORWARD – Mistakes, and Learning from Them iii
PART I – 5 Steps to Doing Well and Feeling Good.........1
   Step #1 – Productivity is the Key...............................2
   Step #2 – The Company's Big Picture.......................6
   Step #3 – Your Individual Contribution...................10
   Step #4 – Have a Willing Attitude 14
   Step #5 – Solve Problems 17
   What If You Don't 23
PART II – 335 Secrets and Tips 27
   1. Relationships..28
   2. Communication 35
   3. Appearance..37
   4. Productivity 39
   5. Organizing Your Work 43
   6. Meetings..46
   7. Company Functions 48
   8. Safety...50
   9. Ethics & Integrity 51
   10. General 53
PART III – Other Important Stuff (OIS) 57
   OIS #1 – 5 Steps – Worksheet 58
   OIS #2 – How to Be at Work on Time.....................60
   OIS #3 – Handling Difficult Customers...................62
   OIS #4 – Supply and Demand..................................64
   OIS #5 – Recommended Reading 66
   OIS #6 – Recommended Learning 67

FORWARD

Mistakes, and Learning from Them

My mother used to tell me that one of the best ways to learn is by making mistakes. Well, I've made a lot of mistakes in my life. And if what my mother said is true, I should have earned myself a Ph.D. by now.

Many of the mistakes I've made, I made at work, and those mistakes have been the most costly. Regrettably, my wife and children suffered the consequences of many of my workplace mistakes. For that, I am truly sorry.

You see, I have a long and rich history of making mistakes at work.

My first experience working outside my parents' home was in the spring of 1964. I was 11 years old and wanted to earn some money to buy a new bike. At dawn one Saturday, my older brother and I rode the farming bus out to the fields on the outskirts of Olympia, Washington. We were going to get rich picking strawberries. We figured, how hard could it be? Some of the people on the bus that morning looked as if they could barely walk, let alone pick. Boy, was I wrong.

Completely exhausted, I quit my first-ever job before I reached my first-ever lunch break. That afternoon, I sat in the shade of a tree waiting for the bus to take me home and wondered, *What is this working thing all about?* No bike was worth that much effort.

A year later, I started baby-sitting. Now there was a job I could enjoy – sitting around, watching TV, raiding the refrigerator. And it paid even better than picking strawberries. If it wasn't for the kids always bothering me, it would have been perfect.

When I was 13, we moved to Alameda, California. In Alameda, I tried something more grown up, something more masculine. I got myself a paper route. But I hated all that lifting and folding, and it paid worse than baby-sitting.

That summer, I heard that the owner of a small carnival at the beach needed someone to help him run the rides. I pictured myself at the controls of the Rock-o-plane or the Tilt-a-whirl. Basking in the sun, I would help beautiful, tanned California girls climb on and off the rides. Yeah, that sounded good. I dropped the paper route for the carnival.

As it turned out, the owner had me running the kiddy rides. My first day, I lifted over 2,000 pounds of small children into and out of the little boats and swings. That job ended before the summer did.

I told everyone that I'd quit so I could concentrate on school. Sure.

In 1970, I graduated from high school and began what I expected to be a long and promising career as a junior college student.

With Vietnam still raging, however, junior college couldn't keep me safe from the draft. The only lottery I've ever won in my life was pulling the number 40 from the Oakland, California draft board, a draft board that had drafted past the number 200 the prior year. Not wanting to carry around a 20 pound backpack and a rifle, I enlisted in the Air Force in 1972 and began my first-ever full-time job.

Over the course of the next ten years, I held many other jobs. I buffed floors, cleaned toilets, repaired computers, and ran a coffee shop. I painted houses, insulated attics, laid tile, and repaired plumbing. I sold things door-to-door, on the phone, face-to-face, and along the side of the road. I was a loan officer, an office manager, a cultist, and a mortgage broker. I ushered for the Padres and took tickets for the Chargers. At one point, I carried $22,000 in cash around in my pockets. At another, I stood in line to collect unemployment. Along the way, I fell in love, got married, and had two children.

Only one thing remained constant. At every job, I made a lot of mistakes.

By 1982, my career had advanced to the point where I was working as a janitor at the VA Hospital in San Diego. At night, I was attending classes at my fourth junior college, and working toward my second AA degree. I wasn't very happy with how my career was progressing, and what I was learning in school didn't seem to be helping much.

Then the hospital laid me off. I'd never lost a job before. I'd always quit first.

I was a 29-year-old, unemployed janitor, husband, and father of two toddlers.

When our daughter was born in 1980, I had promised my wife that if she wanted to be a stay-at-home mom, then I would do whatever it took to provide for us. When the hospital laid me off, our son was only three months old. Our daughter was not yet two and still in diapers. The country was immersed in one of the worst recessions in recent history, and the local unemployment rate was above ten percent.

I was terrified, and so was my wife. The time had arrived for me to figure out what this working thing was all about, but first I had to find myself another job.

For the next two weeks, I frantically studied books on how to find work. I asked everyone I knew if they knew of any job openings. I answered want ads. I sent out resumes. I went on job interviews. I called businesses listed in the yellow pages. I even visited the local retail outlets and strip malls begging for work.

My determination paid off. One of the companies I'd called from the yellow pages offered me a job.

At that time, Bowest Corporation was one of the largest privately owned mortgage servicing companies in the country. From its offices in San Diego, Bowest serviced more than 70,000 mortgages all across the country. And with the country in a recession, Bowest needed help with collections.

Mortgage collections was not glamorous work, but neither was pushing a mop at the VA Hospital. And Bowest paid more, not much more, but more.

So, my wife relaxed, and I went back to work. This time, however, I was determined to figure out how to do it right. At school, I switched my major to business administration. On my own, I started reading books on how to succeed in the corporate world. I also began paying closer attention to the mistakes I made at work, and the mistakes other people made. I cut my hair, started wearing a tie, and changed my attitude.

It worked.

Six years later, I was still working at Bowest, the longest I'd ever worked for any one company. But I was no longer a collector. By the end of 1988, I'd received twelve pay increases, two promotions, was running my own department, and my income had more than tripled. I'd also finished junior college and gone on to earn my bachelor's degree.

More than anything else, though, I'd finally learned some things that helped me to do well and feel good at work. Some of these things I'd studied in school. Some of these things I'd read about in career-advancement books. Some of these things I'd figured out for myself.

I left Bowest in 1989 and set about making a whole new batch of mistakes, first as a business partner, and then later as a business consultant.

Like many people trying to make a living, I wasn't always there for my family. And sometimes when I was there, my mind was somewhere else. Making mistakes ate up a great deal of my time and attention, and I know I missed out on much of what being a father is all about. It's one of my biggest regrets.

When my children started getting their own jobs, I wanted them to do well, of course, but I also wanted to save them from wasting all the time and attention I wasted making mistakes. Time and attention they could better spend with my future grandchildren.

My mother was right when she said making mistakes is one of the best ways to learn, but the most important thing I've learned by making so many mistakes is this:

The **BEST WAY** to learn is from the mistakes of **OTHER PEOPLE**.

My children didn't have to repeat the mistakes I've made to learn from them, and neither do you. That's why I wrote this book. Reflecting on my past 40 years of workplace mistakes, I've isolated 5 steps that helped me do well and feel good at work. I discuss these 5 steps in detail in Part I. If you learn them, I believe you can save yourself a lot of heartache. The first three steps are things you need to learn about work. The fourth is something you need to have. And the fifth is the only thing you actually need to do.

In Part II, I've listed 335 secrets and tips that can help you advance your career. And you just may find (like I did) that advancing your career can improve your life. You'll find some of these suggestions to be obvious, others silly, but all are based on mistakes I've personally made or have seen other people make.

In Part III, I've thrown in some other stuff that doesn't fit in either Part I or Part II, but I think they are important. For example, there's a worksheet to help you apply the 5 steps in Part I to your current job, and instructions on how to be at work on time – every day.

I hope the information in this book helps you as much as it's helped me, and I hope that by learning from my past mistakes, you will not be destined to repeat them.

I've certainly had my share of career failures, but I've also worked hard and achieved some great successes, both as a corporate executive and as an independent business consultant. Without a doubt, successes are better. And being successful has made a huge improvement in my life.

I hope you can use the information in this book to advance your career and improve your life, too.

PART I

THE 5 STEPS TO DOING WELL AND FEELING GOOD AT WORK

> *"To love what you do and feel that it matters —how could anything be more fun?"*
>
> Katharine Graham
> Former Chairman of the Board
> of the Washington Post
> Company

STEP #1

Know that Productivity is the Key to Doing Well and Feeling Good

If you want to do well and feel good at work, your first step is to know that productivity is the key.

Of course there are other things that can make you feel good, like getting a job in the first place. But if you don't produce, you may not feel good for long. In fact, you could lose your job, and that won't feel good at all.

As I mentioned in the Forward, in 1982 I took a job in mortgage collections at Bowest Corporation after being laid-off as a janitor from the VA Hospital. At that time, all new employees of the collections department were assigned to the one-month section. Each month, the collections supervisor gave the one-month section a three-inch thick computer print-out that listed all the people who were late on one mortgage payment. We divided the list among ourselves and called as many of these people as we could each day, asking them to mail in their past due payments.

We were called one-month *counselors*. Probably because somebody thought the term one-month *collector* sounded a bit harsh.

When I started at Bowest, the collections supervisor told me that if I wanted to keep my job, I should make at least 35 phone calls each day. That was the average. I knew that if 35 was the average, then half the counselors must have been making more than 35 calls a day, but the other half must have been making fewer than 35 calls a day. That's what made it an average. I wondered if my new boss was going to fire the half of his staff who called fewer than the average (especially since there would always be half the staff calling fewer than the average), but I decided not to ask.

The collections supervisor also told me I'd probably stay in the one-month section for at least six months. That was fine with me. He also said I shouldn't expect a raise until I'd been with the company for at least a year. I wasn't too happy with that, but I felt good to have gotten the job.

Besides, I figured it couldn't be that hard to make 35 calls a day. Of course, back when I was 11 years old, I didn't think picking strawberries was going to be that hard either. At least I'd be able to sit down while making phone calls.

During my first week at Bowest, I averaged 75 calls a day. It was easier than I'd thought. Only a handful of the people I called each day answered their phones. All I had to do for a *Not-Home* was write *NH* on the computer printout and fill out a postcard asking them to call me back. The whole process of dialing the number, listening to the phone ring ten times (or leaving a message if they had an answering machine), and then filling out a postcard took less than five minutes.

Anyone could have called 75 *Not-Homes* and filled out 75 *Call-Me-Cards* in a day. One call and postcard every five minutes adds up to twelve calls an hour. Twelve calls per hour for eight hours totals 96 calls a day. If I wasn't slowed down by the people who answered their phones and spent time talking to me, my average would have been higher.

Doing more than any other counselor made me feel good. I took comfort in knowing that if a lay-off hit, I'd probably be one of the ones kept around to do the work.

It didn't take long for the collections supervisor to notice that I was averaging twice as many daily calls as the rest of the one-month counselors. By the end of my second month at Bowest, he asked me if I'd be willing to train and *watch over* the other one-month counselors. This wouldn't be a promotion to supervisor, he told me. He just wanted me to do it as a favor. I suspected there might be an opportunity in there somewhere, so I told him I'd be happy to give it a try.

He gave me my first raise four months later. After only six months, I was already doing better financially, and I certainly felt good about that.

If you think about it, doesn't it make sense? The key to you doing well at work, especially doing well enough to be paid more, would have to be productivity. A company can only afford to pay you more money if the value of what you produce for them increases. And, if the overall value of what you produce increases, why wouldn't they want to pay you more? After all, if they don't pay you more, their competitor across the street, or across town, just might.

The collections supervisor could justify raising my hourly rate after just six months because I was already producing more than the employees who had been working there for over a year.

Moving Up

If you apply yourself and become more productive, you'll not only feel better about your job and eventually receive more pay, but at some point you'll advance into a supervisory position, just like what happened to me at Bowest.

By averaging 75 phone calls per day, I was asked to unofficially supervise the other employees in the one-month section. Since the entire collections department only had one official supervisor, my increased responsibilities couldn't be recognized as a formal promotion, and I received no immediate rate increase. However, it did give me the opportunity to show the company that I had management potential.

Since I had greater responsibilities, the collections supervisor gave me permission to work a couple of additional hours of overtime every day. So, although I didn't get a rate increase immediately, I did start making more money because I was working more hours. And since I was paid time-and-a-half for each one of those overtime hours, I considered it a rather nice little raise. Even though the increase only applied to my extra hours, it was a lot more than I would have made if I had taken on a part-time job.

As an unofficial supervisor, I soon learned that productivity was still the key to any future advancement or pay increases. The difference was that, as a supervisor, my productivity was measured by the amount of work done by everyone under my supervision rather than by my work alone.

I didn't realize this at first, and when my individual average dropped from 75 calls per day to less than 50, even though I was working more hours, I got nervous. There didn't seem to be anything I could do about it either. I now had more people I needed to talk to every day. In addition to the people I called who were late on their mortgage payments who happened to answer their phones, I also had to spend time with the other one-month counselors.

The collections supervisor told me to relax. He said an increase in the overall average of the one-month section was more important to him than a drop in my personal average.

Within two months, we raised the average number of daily calls per one-month counselor from 35 to 60. Although my personal average was one of the lowest, the total number of daily calls was higher than it had ever been. The collections supervisor was happy, and I was on my way to earning my first hourly rate increase.

To do well and feel good at work, focus on productivity. As an individual employee, concentrate on increasing your personal productivity. If you move up into a management position, concentrate on helping each of your staff to be more productive.

STEP #2

Know the Company's Big Picture

The second step to doing well and feeling good at work is to know the company's big picture. The big picture is the reason the company exists. What is the company doing? Knowing the big picture will help motivate you as an employee and help you to be more productive.

Most companies exist to make money for their owners, but that's not what I'm talking about. What you want to know is what the company *does* to make money for its owners. And how does that contribute to society?

You might be wondering why you should care how the company contributes to society. You don't *have to* care. Most employees don't. You might just need a job regardless of the company. However, employees who *do* care about how their companies contribute to society tend to have a much higher level of job satisfaction. That's because having an emotional connection to the company helps you feel better about your work. If you have a choice between jobs at two different companies, you should choose the one at the company that excites you the most, even if the pay isn't the highest. You'll feel better and do better in the long run.

Many companies print a mission statement in their employee manuals or in their promotional materials. A mission statement should be the big picture of why the company exists, but it isn't always. Bowest published its mission statement: *The mission of Bowest Corporation is to be the best, not necessarily the biggest.* The best what? It didn't say. I assumed it meant the best mortgage servicing company, but it didn't explain what it meant to be the best mortgage servicing company, or how Bowest was going to be better than all the other mortgage servicing companies.

The only thing Bowest's mission statement did make clear was that being the biggest mortgage servicing company was not part of its mission.

Many companies don't publish mission statements. If the company where you work doesn't have a mission statement, or if their mission statement doesn't clearly state why they exist, then you need to figure it out for yourself. It's up to you to know the company's big picture, even if you're the only person in the entire company who does know it.

To figure out your company's big picture, ask yourself these three questions:

    1. Who is the company trying to help?
    2. What is the company doing to help them?
    3. How do these activities contribute to society?

For example, who was Bowest trying to help? Were we trying to help the people who borrowed the money on their homes, the people I was calling every day? No. The borrowers were not our customers. Our customers were the people who *owned* the mortgage loans. They were the people who had hired Bowest to service those loans.

What did Bowest do to help the people who owned the mortgages? We collected the payments on the loans. We answered the borrowers' questions. Since the collateral for these mortgage loans was the houses the borrowers owned, we made sure the property taxes and fire insurance policies on those houses were paid on time. And we provided reports to the mortgage owners to let them know who still owed them money and how much was owed by each borrower.

How did Bowest's activity contribute to society in general? By taking good care of these loans, we saved the owners of these loans money. They didn't have to foreclose, or pay delinquent taxes or insurance. If mortgage owners made more money, then more people would invest in mortgages. If more people invested in mortgages, then more money would be available to loan to people who wanted to buy houses. And if more money was available to people who wanted to buy houses, then more people would be able to buy houses.

That was Bowest's big picture. By doing a good job servicing mortgages, we were helping people in society buy homes for their families.

Knowing this made me feel better about my job. It helped me stay motivated and be more productive. The truth is, making phone calls and filling out call-me-cards was about as *BORING* as you can imagine. While I worked, however, I kept reminding myself that in addition to earning the money I needed to care for my family, I was also helping other people buy homes. I felt good about that. Someday, I hoped to buy a home as well.

Here's another example. I heard a story some years back about a new supervisor who was watching two of his stone cutters working in a quarry. The new supervisor walked over and asked one of the stone cutters what he was doing.

The stone cutter said, "I'm cutting stone into blocks."

The supervisor then walked over and asked the other stone cutter what he was doing. The other stone cutter pointed into the distance and said, "We're part of the construction team building that new cathedral over there."

The first stone cutter had given the supervisor a straightforward answer, accurate and obvious. But his answer didn't explain the big picture, did it? The second stone cutter's answer, however, was a simple and complete statement of the big picture. He knew why he was cutting stone into blocks.

Which one of those stone cutters do you think was the more motivated, made the better decisions, and stayed more productive? Which one do you think was most likely to become a supervisor? And, if you were building a cathedral, which one would you want cutting stones for you?

That's why you need to know the big picture. It helps you stay motivated and productive. You feel good about the work you're doing because you know that you're contributing to a much larger activity, even if the only thing you're actually doing is cutting stone into blocks or calling people who are late on their mortgage payments.

Knowing the big picture can also help you decide if the company you work for is the right company for you. For example, if you feel that smoking is bad for people, you shouldn't work for a tobacco company, or a company that makes cigarette lighters.

You'll feel better about yourself, your job, and your life if you only work for a company whose big picture is something you completely support. If you have a passion for what the company does, that's even better.

STEP #3

Know Your Individual Contribution to the Company's Big Picture

The third step to doing well and feeling good at work is to know your contribution to the company's big picture. Your contribution to the company's big picture is the reason why your position exists inside the company. What are you supposed to be doing, and how does that activity help the company help others?

As an employee, you are part of a team, and every member of that team has duties and responsibilities. In order for the company to succeed, it must be productive. In order for the company to be productive, each member of the team must be productive.

In other words, how does your activity help the company? The answer to that question will clarify your individual responsibilities and help you decide what to do first.

For example, Bowest took care of mortgages for the investors who owned the loans. That was their big picture. One of the many things the company did to take care of those loans was to make sure the borrowers paid their payments on time.

Making sure the borrowers paid their payments on time was the duty and responsibility of the collections department. The collections department didn't pay property taxes. We didn't pay insurance premiums. We didn't prepare reports for the investors. All those duties and responsibilities were assigned to other departments. Our primary responsibility was to make sure the borrowers paid their payments on time.

The collections department was divided into areas. In the one-month area, we called borrowers late on one payment.

We didn't call borrowers late on two or more payments. Other sections made those phone calls.

Within the one-month area, my personal job was to call the borrowers listed on the section of the printout assigned to me. That was the first thing I was supposed to do.

Why did my job as a one-month counselor exist inside Bowest? Because the company knew that if someone picked up the phone and called the people who were late on one payment, most of those people would send in their payments. If no one called, then more borrowers would be late on two payments at the beginning of the next month. In the long run, calling people reduced the number of delinquencies. That reduced the number of foreclosures. And that reduced the costs to the investors who owned the mortgages.

My calling borrowers late on one payment helped Bowest be the best mortgage servicing company in the country (even though we weren't necessarily the biggest).

Here's another example. Suppose I took a job as a mail clerk at Microsoft, one of the largest software manufacturers in the world. As a mail clerk, why would my position exist inside Microsoft, and what would be my contribution to their big picture? My position would exist to ensure Microsoft's mail was distributed timely, right? And Microsoft's big picture might be to develop and sell affordable business and personal software to improve their customers' productivity and enjoyment with personal computers. Something like that.

So, how would my job as the mail clerk contribute to the big picture at Microsoft? Could Microsoft sell and deliver their software if their mail wasn't distributed? By distributing the mail, I'd be helping the sales people know who wants to buy. I'd be helping the shipping clerks know what to ship. Basically, I'd be helping the rest of the staff do their jobs.

Now let's suppose I became a mail clerk for Alaska Airlines. There, my personal contribution to the big picture would be similar, but my company's big picture would be quite different. At Alaska Airlines, my contribution to the big picture would still be to ensure the mail was distributed timely, but now I'd be contributing to the transportation of people and cargo safely and efficiently by plane as opposed to supporting the development, sales, and distribution of software. It's the same contribution, but a different big picture.

What to do First

Knowing your contribution to the company's big picture helps you to decide what to do first.

As a one-month counselor, my primary focus was to call the people listed on my section of the printout who were late on one mortgage payment. I started working at Bowest in the middle of August of 1982 and went right to work making phone calls.

On the first day of September, however, there was no one for me to call.

All of the borrowers had been given a 15-day grace period as part of their loan contracts. So, their payments weren't considered late until the 16th of the month. During the first half of each month, no one was late on just one payment. Either their payment wasn't past due yet, or they owed two or more payments.

Therefore, for half of each month, there appeared to be no reason for my position as a one-month counselor to exist. If I called people before the 16th who weren't technically late on their payments, I wouldn't be contributing to the overall productivity of the company. In fact, calling before the 16th would be a waste of my time and the company's money (not to mention more than a little upsetting to the borrowers).

After two weeks of making 75 phone calls per day, I felt a little lost not having anyone to call. How was I supposed to be productive? I soon learned that the collections department had other work for me to do.

My secondary job as a one-month counselor turned out to be helping the two-month counselors get organized. Since the two-month counselors called people late on two payments, they didn't have to wait to call their borrowers. The two-month counselors were on the phones every day, all month.

On the first day of each month, the two-month counselors handed over all the files they had left from the previous month to the counselors in the pre-foreclosure area because those borrowers were now late on three payments. At the same time, the two-month counselors needed all the files for the people who were now late on two payments.

The one-month counselors worked from printouts, not files. So, part of our job was to pull files for the two-month counselors. If a collection file didn't already exist for a borrower (either it was a new loan, or the borrowers had never been late on two payments before), then we would create a new file. By having us handle the files, the two-month counselors were able to stay on the phones.

On the 16th of September, however, the focus of the one-month counselors switched back to our primary duty of making phone calls. If a two-month counselor asked me to pull a file during the last half of the month, I had to politely decline. After the 16th, they were expected to pull their own files. If I didn't do my primary job of making phone calls during the last half of the month, the two-month counselors would have more work at the beginning of the next month.

By knowing how my individual activities contributed to Bowest's big picture, I understood my primary responsibility and what I needed to do first.

STEP #4

Have a Willing Attitude

The *most important* step to doing well and feeling good at work is to have a willing attitude.

If you don't have enough education, you can be taught what to do. If you don't have enough experience, you can be coached on how to do your job. However, if you're not *willing* to try your best, if you're not *willing* to learn from your mistakes, if you're not *willing* to take direction and advice, then forget about it. No one can help you.

The first three steps are designed to help you develop a willing attitude. If you understand that the key to doing well and feeling good at work is productivity, and if you know and agree with your company's big picture, and if you know and agree with your individual contribution to that big picture, then you should have a willing attitude.

As a business consultant, whenever a client tells me they're having difficulty with an employee, the first thing I have them evaluate is the employee's attitude. Is that employee willing? If my client doesn't think the employee *clearly* demonstrates a willing attitude, I immediately recommend they terminate that employee, regardless of anything else.

How can you possibly be productive in the long run if you're not willing to work? And whether or not you have a willing attitude is determined by your actions, not your words. It's what you do that matters, not what you say.

1. How do you react when your supervisor asks you to do something extra? Do you whine about it not being fair? Do you say that someone else should have to do it? Or do you just start doing what was asked of you?

2. What do you do when you see something wrong? Do you complain to whoever will listen, or do you bring it to the attention of your supervisor and suggest a way to fix it?
3. How's the quality of your work? Do you do the best work possible within the time available, or does someone else have to fix what you've done to make it acceptable?
4. How much work do you get done? Are you productive, or do you accomplish less than average?
5. How much time and attention do you devote to your responsibilities? Are you focused and efficient throughout the day, or do you waste time with personal phone calls and continuous breaks?
6. And finally, how do you treat the other employees at the company? Are you respectful and willing to help others, or do you gossip and stir up trouble?

All of these actions show your attitude, regardless of anything you might say.

Why would anyone accept a job at a company and be unwilling to work? I've seen it hundreds of times and still don't understand it. These people are never happy. I suspect they're unwilling to work because they lack one or all of the first three steps. They don't understand that productivity is the key to doing well and feeling good at work. Or they don't know or want to be a part of the company's big picture. Or they don't like their supervisor and don't want to support that supervisor's contribution to the company's big picture. Or perhaps they just have personal problems.

I don't know what's wrong with them, but I do know that if you ever find yourself in a similar situation, it's time to go find yourself another job. Do it before you're fired.

Confucius once said, "Find a job you love to do, and you'll never have to work a day in your life." This statement is mostly true, but it's missing three other important parts.

First, you not only have to love what you do, but you also have to be good at it, or at least be able to get good at it. It doesn't matter how much you love to sing, if you can't carry a tune, and you don't have the physical ability to eventually be able to carry a tune, then singing would not be a good job for you.

Second, even if you are good at your job, someone has to be willing to pay you to do it. It won't matter if you can sing fantastically, if no one is willing to pay you to sing, then singing would still not be a good job for you.

And third, the job can't be something that your conscious tells you not to do. Let's say you sing great, and you finally find someone who is willing to pay you to sing, but they want you to sing naked. If your conscious tells you that singing naked isn't right, then even that job would not be good for you.

All four parts are essential to having a great career.

If you *can* find a job that you love, are good at, pays you well, and is aligned with your conscious, then there will be no stopping you. You will be destined to succeed.

If you spend eight hours a day at a job, that represents one third of your life, which is half of the time you are awake. If you're going to invest that much of your life in something, be sure it's something you love to do, or at least something you like to do. Don't continue to get up every morning when you don't want to get up; so you can go somewhere you don't want to go; to do something you don't want to do; with people you don't like.

What kind of a life is that?

Instead, find a job where you're excited about getting up in the morning. Where you love the work you do and the people you work with. Even if that job doesn't pay as well as other jobs at first, the benefits will more than make up the difference.

STEP #5

Solve Problems

The only thing you actually need to do in order to do well and feel good at work is solve problems. As an employee, your only job is to solve problems for the company.

What problem for Bowest was I trying to solve as a one-month counselor? Bowest knew that some borrowers wouldn't make their payments if we didn't call them. That was a problem. If borrowers got behind on one payment, it was easy to get behind on two, or three. Once they were that far behind, it was far more difficult for them to ever catch up. And if that happened, more loans would end up in foreclosure, an expensive and time consuming process. When loans went into foreclosure, the borrowers lost their homes, and the investors lost part of their investment. That was a problem.

My job was to help solve that problem by encouraging people to mail in their one late payment.

Why would Microsoft or Alaska Airlines bother to hire mail clerks? Both companies have a problem. People keep writing to them, and the post office keeps dumping all this mail on their doorsteps. That's a problem for them. They need someone to solve it. They need someone to sort through all that mail and deliver it to the right people inside their companies. If the mail isn't delivered, customer orders aren't filled, bills aren't paid, and neither company can make money or contribute to society.

As an employee, what problems are you responsible for? You are responsible for all the problems that relate to your position inside the company. That's why it's so important for you to clearly understand your contribution to the company's big picture, so you can solve the problems associated with it.

As a one-month counselor, I was responsible for calling as many people as I could during the last half of the month and helping the two-month counselors call as many people as they could during the first half of the month.

I remember my first day on the phones. I was taught to call a late borrower and wait for ten rings to see if they answered the phone. If they didn't, and most didn't, then I was to fill out a call-me-card and dial the next number on my list. I was so bored listening to the phone ring and then filling out those silly postcards. I made 40 calls that first day, but the work was much too slow. It drove me crazy.

I wasn't the only one. I noticed that some of the other one-month counselors seemed to find any excuse to get up and wander around the office. If I was going to keep my new job, I had to find some way to speed things up.

The next day, I timed the telephone rings and discovered that ten rings took almost a minute. If I was going to average 35 calls a day, that meant I would have to sit at my desk and listen to the phone ring for over half an hour each day. Not my idea of a good time. Next, I timed myself filling out a call-me-card. That also took about a minute. Perfect.

I started filling out my call-me-cards while the phone rang. I'd fill out everything except the borrower's name and address. Now I had something to do rather than count the rings. I set my watch on my desk. After about a minute, if no one answered the phone, I'd hang up and dial my next number. While that phone rang, I'd fill out the name and address of my last call on the call-me-card and then fill out most of the information on another. If no one answered the phone by the time I was done, I'd hang up and call another. By doing this, I kept the phone calls going without stopping to write. It also gave me something to do while the phone rang.

I made a game out of it. How many calls could I make in one day? Each day, I tried to do better than the last.

Because I dialed the phone more times each day than the other one-month counselors, I also contacted more borrowers, did more actual counseling, and got more people to send in their past due payments. This reduced the amount of work I had to transfer to the two-month area the next month, thereby reducing their workload. Everyone benefited.

I was the first one-month counselor at Bowest to call every borrower on my list. When I finished, I called the borrowers at the end of another one-month counselor's list that he didn't have time to call.

My primary focus was on solving the problems related to my contribution to the one-month area, and the one-month area's contribution to the company's big picture. In doing so, I also helped solve problems for the two-month area.

The problems of the one-month area were what I needed to solve first because that was my primary contribution to the company's big picture. If I'd been a mail clerk, I wouldn't have tried to increase the productivity of the one-month counselors, I would have tried to improve the efficiency of the mail room.

I read a story years ago about an assembly line worker at General Motors. He noticed a problem with all the different sized cotter pins he had to use to attach the different car parts on the assembly line. He thought it would be a lot easier if all the parts of the car that needed cotter pins were attached with the same size pin. It wasn't his job to design cotter pins, but they were causing him a problem. So, he suggested the company standardize the size of the cotter pins.

According to the story, General Motors investigated it and found that assembly line workers in all their plants were having problems with the cotter pins, and that standardizing the sizes was a great solution to the problem. Not only did standardizing the sizes save time on assembly lines all over the world, but it also saved money in the manufacturing and storage of the cotter pins since they were now all the same size.

That one suggestion saved General Motors millions of dollars over the next several years. For his suggestion, they paid that assembly line worker a commission of $250,000.

As an employee, you have a unique perspective on the work that needs to be done in your area and the problems associated with that work. No one else in the company is doing your exact job. They may be doing similar jobs, but not your exact job. Therefore, you see things differently than anyone else. Because of that, you might see a problem that no one else sees. You can use that problem as an opportunity for yourself by bringing it to your supervisor's attention.

Before you tell your supervisor about it, study the problem thoroughly until you understand it. In Part II, tip #314, I mention that every problem contains its own solution. If you study a problem until you understand it completely, the solution will become obvious. By studying what was boring about making phone calls, I was able to figure out a different procedure that kept me interested in the work. By studying the cotter pin problem, the GM employee found a simple solution.

Once you understand the problem, then present your supervisor with *both* an explanation of the problem and at least one recommended solution. Even if your solution isn't the one that's used, you'll be exercising your problem solving skills and demonstrating your willingness to try.

While at work, mentally set your personal life and your personal problems aside. Keep all of your attention on being productive and solving the company's problems. If you do that, you'll do great.

Everyone's Job is to Solve Problems

If you look at the employees inside any company, you'll find that their only job is to solve problems. That includes every employee from mail clerk to president.

The only difference between the job of mail clerk and the job of president is the size and complexity of the problems they solve for the company. The mail clerk solves problems relating to getting the mail delivered. The president solves problems relating to keeping the entire company productive and profitable.

Have you ever noticed that the bigger the problems a person solves, the bigger their paycheck tends to be? Always tackle the biggest problems you can. You might surprise yourself how capable you really are, and how quickly you could move into management.

But keep this in mind; solve the problems relating to your primary contribution to the company's big picture *first*. No supervisor wants to hear suggestions on how to run the company better from someone whose own area is a mess. Solve your own production problems before you tackle the problems in another area.

Don't be a Problem

As an employee, you have a choice. You can either *solve* problems for your company (the reason you were hired), or you will *be* a problem for your company.

Have you ever heard someone say that a particular company or department had an *Employee Problem*? Or, have you ever known of an employee who was referred to as a problem? Does that make any sense?

People are hired to solve problems, not to be problems.

How does an employee become a problem? They don't follow these five steps. They don't understand that productivity is the key to doing well and feeling good at work. They either don't know, or don't agree with, the company's big picture. They don't know, or don't agree with, their contribution to the company's big picture. They don't have a willing attitude. Or they don't focus their attention on solving the problems that relate to their area.

When that happens, they become a problem the company has to solve.

Don't Expect Problem Solving
to be a Smooth Ride

Things seldom go smoothly in any workplace. Companies exist in the world. The world is unpredictable. People inhabit the workplace. People are unpredictable. That's why employees are needed to help companies solve problems.

Some problems are predictable, like mail delivery. Some problems are unpredictable, like an economic crisis, or the damage that can be caused by a disgruntled employee or a natural disaster. Things are always changing at work. Expect things to change, and solve the problems that are brought about by things changing. If you don't, then you could become part of the things that are changed (you could be fired).

During my first year in the collections department at Bowest, I moved from the one-month area to the two-month area and finally into the pre-foreclosure area. Along the way, I analyzed and streamlined the procedures for each position I held. Eventually, I provided the collections supervisor with suggestions on how he could better run the department.

During my annual review, the collections supervisor suggested I find employment elsewhere. I was dumb-struck. The collections department was operating better than ever. Delinquencies were down, and I thought I'd helped him look good. Yet, he wanted me to leave. I wasn't fired. In fact, he gave me another raise, but he told me I had no future in his department, and he refused to explain.

The only thing I could imagine was that he must have felt threatened in some way by my presence in his department. He'd been the collections supervisor for a number of years, and I don't think he had any aspiration to advance further in the company. But he knew I did, and I guess he might have been worried about me taking his job.

Perhaps he was aware of the old saying, "Even if you're on the right track, you can still be run over if you don't keep moving." I must have been moving up behind him a little too quickly for his comfort.

Whatever the reason, I soon transferred to the commercial loan servicing department. There, I solved problems for a supervisor who didn't feel threatened by me.

After three years in commercial loan servicing, I transferred to corporate accounting where I was eventually promoted to Vice President and Controller of the company.

What If You Don't...

If You Don't Know Step #1

If you don't know that productivity is the key to doing well and feeling good at work, then you won't be focused on being productive. You may work hard to fit in, or try to get to know the right people, or search for the best opportunity. But that focus isn't going to sustain you in the long run.

Eventually, you're going to feel inadequate and overpaid. You'll start looking over your shoulder for who might be creeping up behind you, wondering when your boss is going to find out that you're not worthy. And you won't be doing well or feeling good about your work.

It's far better to focus on being productive. Productivity will validate your worth. You'll feel more confident and secure in your ability. And you won't have to worry about losing your job. Even if something happens to the company, you'll know that other companies always need productive people. So, regardless of what happens, you'll always be able to find a job somewhere.

If You Don't Know Step #2

If you don't know the company's big picture, you can have trouble keeping yourself motivated, and you'll tend to be less productive.

No job is fun all the time. Everyone has to do some boring or unpleasant tasks. But you can keep yourself going by knowing that what you do contributes to the company's big picture, especially if that company's big picture is something you completely support.

When I worked at the VA Hospital, I was occasionally asked to mop the operating room floor. Now that was a totally disgusting task.

However, I knew the doctors couldn't save anyone's life if they were slipping around on the blood from their last operation. By mopping the floor, I helped the doctors help others. It was still a disgusting task, but I was motivated to do it and do it well. Between mopping the operating room floor and sweeping the stairwell, mopping the operating room was the more important task. Even though sweeping the stairwell was far less disgusting, mopping the operating room contributed more to the VA Hospital's big picture.

If You Don't Know Step #3

If you don't know your contribution to the company's big picture, you can have trouble knowing what to do first.

While you're at work, you should stay focused on that which is the most important task at the moment. If you don't, then you won't be as productive as you should be.

While I was a one-month counselor, if I'd been helping the two-month counselors during the last half of the month, I would have been doing the wrong task. My primary job focus was to call borrowers who were late on one payment. Helping the two-month counselors was my secondary focus. If I didn't call borrowers who were late on one payment, the two-month counselors would have been swamped the next month because more borrowers would then be late on two payments simply because I hadn't called them.

If a mail clerk is too busy talking to the sales and marketing department about a new ad campaign, then the mail isn't getting delivered. If the mail isn't delivered, then the sales and marketing department won't receive the customer orders. If the sales and marketing department doesn't receive the customer orders, the company's products don't help any customers. And if the company's products don't help any customers, a new ad campaign isn't needed because the company will be going out of business.

If You Don't Have Step #4 or Do Step #5

If you don't have a willing attitude, or don't solve problems, then you'll produce nothing. You'll contribute nothing to the company or society. And you'll become a problem that the company will need to solve. Eventually, you'll be unemployed.

And then, finding a new job will be the next problem you'll need to solve. If that happens to you, reread these 5 steps to doing well and feeling good at work.

If You Do, It Does Get Better

In 1989, I left Bowest and went to work for a real estate research and consulting firm. I became a partner the following year, but left after three years. What I learned from the mistakes I made as a business partner could fill a whole other book, maybe two.

I'm much happier on my own as a business consultant. And I still follow these same five steps with each of my clients.

1. I know the key to my doing well and feeling good is my productivity. If I don't work, I don't get paid. And if I don't get paid, I don't feel too good.
2. With each new client, I ask myself, "What's their big picture?"
3. I then figure out what my contribution will be to their big picture.
4. I maintain a willing attitude, always trying to help them in any way I can.
5. And I do everything possible to help solve their problems.

I've been involved in a wide variety of problem solving for my clients. I've analyzed other businesses for acquisition, taught financial analysis, set up accounting systems, reconciled accounts, interviewed prospective employees, trained current employees, filled out bank deposit slips, printed checks, filed papers, even fixed stuck desk drawers. Whatever was needed to be done, I did.

One afternoon, I even examined a cut on the bottom of a client's foot to see if there was glass in it. Why would I do that? Because she was paying me to help her with her business. She was in pain. And she asked me to look at her foot. How effective can a business owner be if she has glass stuck in the bottom of her foot? So, I looked at it. That's what having a willing attitude is all about.

There are only three types of people in this world:
    1. People who make things happen.
    2. People who watch things happen.
    3. People who wonder, *what happened?*

Whenever you're on the job, follow these five steps. Stay motivated, stay focused, and solve problems. Solve problems for yourself. Solve problems for your company. And solve problems for the people around you. If you do, you'll never be left to wonder what happened.

PART II

335 SECRETS AND TIPS TO ADVANCE YOUR CAREER (WHICH MIGHT HELP IMPROVE YOUR LIFE)

> *"If a man is called to be a street sweeper, he should sweep streets even as Michelangelo painted, or Beethoven composed music, or Shakespeare wrote poetry. He should sweep streets so well that all the hosts of heaven and earth will pause to say, here lived a great street sweeper who did his job well."*
>
> Dr. Martin Luther King, Jr.
> Main Leader of the American Civil Rights Movement

1. RELATIONSHIPS

Relationships are the foundation of all businesses. To succeed, a company strives to establish long lasting, mutually beneficial relationships with customers, staff, vendors, owners, and everyone else associated with the company. How well a company handles its relationships determines if that company succeeds or fails.

How well you handle your relationships at work determines if your career advances, stagnates, or disappears.

1. Don't cook fish in the company microwave, broccoli either. They stink when cooked.
2. Clean up your own messes, and wash your dishes and coffee cups. Don't make someone else have to clean up after you.
3. Don't litter, including cigarette butts. It makes unnecessary work for other people. See #2.
4. Smile. If you're feeling good about your work, which you should if you're following the five steps in Part I, then show it and you can brighten everyone else's day.
5. Always keep your word. It's called having integrity. Relationships are built on trust. If you don't have integrity, then you won't be trusted because you aren't trust*worthy*.
6. When you make a mistake, sincerely apologize and offer to fix it. And apologize immediately. Don't wait around hoping you won't have to.
7. Be quick to forgive and forget your co-workers' transgressions.
8. Help your co-workers, even if you don't like them – especially if you don't like them.
9. Treat others as you'd like to be treated.
10. Think before you act. Your first impulse may not be your best.

11. Be tolerant of your co-workers' bad habits.
12. Hold the door and elevator for others.
13. Get permission before borrowing anything from someone else's desk or area.
14. Return what you borrow when you stop using it. Borrow it again later if needed.
15. If you find yourself borrowing something regularly, request one for yourself.
16. Remember people's names. The less important someone is in a company, the more important it is to remember their name. When introduced to someone, it helps to repeat their name to yourself. Write it down later if necessary.
17. When you meet people that you have already been introduced to, say hello and mention your name – assume they have forgotten it.
18. Pick your battles carefully and don't try to win every disagreement. Only hold out for those things most important to you and allow your opponents to win the others.
19. Be gracious in both victory and defeat.
20. Don't park in a spot that is reserved for someone else.
21. Try not to do or say anything that might offend someone.
22. Keep your body clean and odor free.
23. Don't overdo it with your perfume, aftershave, or cologne.
24. If you must smoke on your drive to work, roll down the windows. If you leave the windows up, you'll smell like stale smoke for hours.
25. Don't smoke around people who are bothered by it – and always ask first.
26. Never tell jokes that poke fun at age, race, gender, physical limitations, social or ethnic background, political or religious affiliation, or anything of a sexual nature.

27. When other staff members arrive at work, avoid looking at your watch. In 1984, I had a habit of looking at my watch when my co-worker arrived each morning. I wanted to know how much I'd gotten done before eight o'clock, but my co-worker thought I was reporting the time he arrived to our supervisor. When he told me why he disliked me, I stopped looking at my watch and we started getting along better.
28. Never gloat – especially about how productive you are.
29. Never offer a handshake, or a hug, to a female co-worker unless she offers it to you first. Unless she's choking, of course.
30. Don't hug someone, or squeeze their hand, tighter than they're squeezing you back.
31. Keep air-freshener handy, and use it sparingly if needed.
32. When you praise someone, do it when other people are around.
33. Show enthusiasm whenever a co-worker does well or is promoted.
34. Never discuss your pay, or anyone else's pay, with your co-workers. If you do, there are only three possible outcomes: One, you're paid less. If that happens, you'll feel bad because you'll think you deserve at least as much. Two, you're paid more, and then they'll feel bad for the same reason. Three, you're both paid the same. In which case, you'll both feel bad, each of you believing you deserve more than the other.
35. Don't eat garlic or onions before or at work.
36. Don't gossip or spread rumors.
37. Repeat compliments you hear about others.
38. Be polite. Use please and thank you.
39. Say excuse me and I'm sorry whenever needed – and mean it.

40. Be nice to everyone you contact.
41. Be as courteous to the receptionist as you are to the President.
42. Practice humility.
43. Don't worry if someone else gets credit for something you did. But if it happens regularly, find a way to leak the truth. See #73.
44. When you receive recognition for something you did, be sure to acknowledge everyone who helped you get it done.
45. Avoid one-upping your co-workers. After they finish talking, don't try to tell a funnier story, or a scarier experience, let them have their moment.
46. Don't call one of the company's executives or customers by their first name unless they give you permission. It's better to show someone too much respect rather than not enough. How they introduce themselves may indicate how they wish to be addressed.
47. Don't give advice to co-workers unless asked.
48. Don't assume you know what is wrong with someone else.
49. Don't talk behind other peoples' backs. This includes former employers and co-workers.
50. Don't trust anyone who talks to you behind other people's backs. You can be sure they're talking about you behind your back.
51. Put the toilet seat down when you're finished.
52. In a crisis, do more than anyone would expect.
53. Help and support your co-workers – they may someday be your employees or supervisor, and they'll remember how you treated them.
54. If you upset a co-worker, be willing to apologize – even if you don't think it was your fault. And mean it when you say it.
55. Don't bring your children's fund raisers to work. Your co-workers might resent it.

56. If a co-worker brings a baby, or photographs of a baby, into the office, find something about it you can say looks cute. This applies to pets as well, maybe more so.
57. Only car pool with people who hold the same opinions you do about work.
58. When carpooling, don't smoke on the way to work. Even with the windows rolled down, you'll all end up smelling like stale smoke.
59. When carpooling, unless you can all agree on a station, don't turn on the radio.
60. When angry, avoid confrontations – especially physical confrontations. Taking a walk can help you calm down, as long as you walk *away* from the person you're mad at.
61. Never push or shove anyone. It's called *Battery* as in *Assault and Battery*.
62. Try to make your boss look good. You could have the same boss for a long time.
63. Turn in your expense reports on time – with receipts attached.
64. Don't try to control other staff members – strive to understand them.
65. Perform unexpected acts of kindness.
66. Never say anything that sounds like, "That's what you told me to do." It sounds like you're blaming them for something you did. It's better to say something apologetic and responsible like, "I'm sorry. That's what I thought I was supposed to do. What should I do instead?"
67. Keep your personal plans for your future personal. Discuss them only with family members and your closest friends.
68. Only accept those secrets from others that you will keep to yourself.
69. Only tell secrets of your own that you're willing to have repeated.

70. Never betray a confidence. Don't discuss with others anything someone told you to keep private – especially company secrets.
71. Only discuss sensitive matters in private. Be aware that the people around you might be able to hear what you're saying.
72. Learn how to perform artificial respiration, CPR, the Heimlich maneuver, and basic first aid. Nothing strengthens relationships better than saving someone's life.
73. Don't boast. Have someone else let people know how well you're doing. When I graduated from college, my wife threw a surprise party for me at Bowest and invited all the managers. At the party, they learned I'd graduated with honors without me having to boast about it. Remember, you'll never be able to toot your own horn as loud or as effectively as someone else can.
74. Don't crowd people. Everyone is surrounded by their own private space, if you move in too close, they'll feel uncomfortable.
75. Keep a set of jumper cables in your car – in case someone else needs them. And have a properly inflated spare tire and a jack for yourself.
76. Never get romantically involved with your boss or your subordinates.
77. If you date a co-worker, be careful. The success or failure in that relationship will end your working environment as you know it. Whether your co-worker eventually becomes your spouse or your ex-lover, dealing with them at work will become increasingly more complicated as your relationship changes.
78. Keep your love life outside of the workplace. That means no kissing, no hand holding, no

love-note passing, no affectionate staring, and no sly winking.
79. Regardless of what you accomplish in your life, never treat other people as if you are better than them – especially if you are better than them.

Avoid Embarrassing Others

80. Don't do *anything* you think might embarrass someone – whether you think it's funny or not.
81. Compliment other people's work, but never their appearance or weight. Even a perfectly worded compliment about how someone looks can be misinterpreted.
82. Never correct someone if other people are around. Get them alone first.
83. Don't refer to family members by family names. For example, don't tell the son of the President that his *Dad* wants to see him.
84. When you disagree with someone, don't be insulting. Show them more respect than usual while you explain your opposing viewpoint.
85. Don't ask co-workers personal questions until after you get to know them.
86. How and when you say something is just as important as what you say. Always deliver unpleasant communication tactfully, in the right way and at the right time.
87. If you give copies of this book to co-workers (or your boss), don't highlight the parts you want them to notice – unless you give it to them anonymously.

2. COMMUNICATION

Communication is the foundation of every relationship.

88. Know that the purpose of communication is understanding.
89. Spend at least twice as much time listening as you do talking.
90. Be interest*ed* in the person you're with – don't try to be interest*ing* to them.
91. Listen with empathy. Try to see the world as the person talking sees it.
92. Look people in the eye when communicating.
93. Don't wear tinted glasses indoors unless you are required to do so by your doctor.
94. Understand what the other person is saying before you attempt to get them to understand what you want to say. In his book *The 7 Habits of Highly Effective People*, Stephen R. Covey refers to this as Habit #5 – Seek First to Understand, Then to Be Understood.
95. Focus more on what is being said rather than on who is saying it.
96. When someone is talking to you, don't interrupt, don't judge, and don't think about your response – just *listen*.
97. When someone tells you a tragic, personal story, say, "I am so sorry," rather than, "I know how you feel." They won't think you do.
98. Be sure you understand instructions before you attempt to follow them. Don't nod your head and pretend you understand when you don't.
99. If possible, keep your voice soft and low.
100. Use common words, and avoid using jargon with anyone who might not understand it.

101. Be accurate and specific. Exaggerations and generalities hinder understanding.
102. Think before you talk. Your first thought is seldom your best. This doesn't apply during brainstorming sessions where you want a free flow of ideas.
103. Avoid using bad language.
104. Keep your email to one page or less. Abraham Lincoln could fit the Gettysburg Address on one page. Your message should fit, too.
105. When you write something, stick to the facts and avoid assumptions and opinions.
106. Use a font that is easy to read. 12-point Arial and Times New Roman are my favorites.
107. Use white space liberally around paragraphs, tables, and related information.
108. Don't send a copy of your email to anyone who doesn't need to see it. Just because it's easy for you to cc everyone, it might still be a waste of their time to read it.
109. Smile when you answer the phone. The person on the other end can hear it in your voice.
110. When you answer the company's phone, say something like, "Good morning, Ajax Company. This is Tim Shortridge."
111. When you answer your own phone inside the company, "This is Tim Shortridge," is fine.
112. If you can't help someone on the phone, offer to take a message and have someone get back to them. Then have someone get back to them.
113. Become the best message taker in your area. Write down the caller's name, the date and time they called, their company name, why they called, and if they need a return call.
114. If you're not sure what to say, say nothing.

3. APPEARANCE

Every day, your appearance is the first thing you communicate to the people in your workplace. It says volumes about who you are, even if you wish it didn't.

115. Dress appropriately for your job. What you wear should blend in with what everyone else wears. If you're working in a professional office, a suit might be appropriate. But if you're working in construction, a suit wouldn't be appropriate.
116. Dress for your co-workers, not yourself. You may not care how you look, but it's your co-workers who have to look at you all day.
117. Don't wear clothing or jewelry that might draw attention to yourself. You're there to work, not distract people.
118. If you must wear something outrageous, wear outrageous underwear – that no one can see.
119. Keep your hair clean, neat, and trimmed.
120. Keep your tattoos covered.
121. Keep a toothbrush in your car or purse, and brush your teeth after you eat. But before you arrive at work. Floss is also a good idea. It works better than a toothpick, won't break off between your teeth, and doesn't make you look like a hoodlum when you use it. But don't use either while you're at work.
122. While at work, don't make yourself at home.
123. Never criticize the company or its employees while at work. Do that later with your friends.
124. Walk quickly and with purpose – don't dawdle.
125. Don't chew gum or tobacco at work. You'll look like you have an attitude.
126. Don't spit.

127. Never play games (computer or otherwise) at your desk or work station. Even if you're on a break, it looks like you're fooling around on company time.
128. Never read personal mail, magazines, or a novel at your desk or work station. For the same reason as #127.
129. Don't watch the clock. It looks like you don't like being there and can't wait to leave.
130. Don't be in a hurry to rush out the door at the end of the day. Work until your shift is over, then clean your area before you leave.
131. Be as good of an employee as you can – even if you're the only one on staff trying to be a good employee.
132. Do all personal grooming in the restroom. This includes, but is not limited to, tugging on your undershorts, combing your hair, filing or clipping your nails, refreshing your make-up, brushing your teeth, or flossing.
133. Don't take reading material with you to the restroom.
134. Pick up any litter you see around the company.
135. Be sure you're alone before scratching or picking at any part of your body.
136. Don't use the entrance to the company as a smoking area.
137. Never allow anything to stick out of your nostrils.
138. Always carry a tissue or handkerchief. So you can offer it to someone else, or you discover that you're in violation of #137.

4. PRODUCTIVITY

The purpose of the workplace is to produce. That's why you're there.

139. Earn your rewards. Forget the idea that anyone owes you a living.
140. Don't bother to learn how to get by. Learn how to get the work done.
141. Love your work. Develop a passion for your individual contribution to your company.
142. Always do your best.
143. Supervise yourself. Don't force someone else to tell you when to start or what to do.
144. Find someone who has already had a successful career doing what you want to do, then do what they did. Anthony Robbins discusses this at length in his book *Unlimited Power*.
145. Learn from the best until you are the best, then teach others.
146. Do each task right the first time. It's far easier than going back later to fix it.
147. Do one thing at a time. Put all your attention on it until it's done.
148. Know when a task is done. Then stop working on it, and move on to the next.
149. Don't slow down because you're afraid you'll run out of work. Find more to do, outside your department if necessary. Always have a long-range project you can work on, possibly something no one else wants to do.
150. Don't assume the way you're taught to do a task is the best way to do it. But learn to do it that way *before* you suggest improvements.

151. Take the stairs if they're quicker than the elevator. You'll save time and benefit from the exercise.
152. Treat escalators as stairs. You'll reach the top faster.
153. If you've completed all your work, ask your supervisor for more. The best way to ask is, "What else can I do to help you?" If your supervisor is unavailable, help someone else in your area while you wait.
154. Realize that the more you know, the more you can solve complicated problems. And that makes you more productive and valuable.
155. Nurture your curiosity. Ask yourself why, then investigate.
156. Continue your education. Whether you take college courses, study books, or read magazines, never stop learning. In *The 7 Habits of Highly Effective People*, Stephen R. Covey refers to this as Habit #7 – Sharpen the Saw.
157. During on-the-job-training, listen carefully, understand completely, and observe someone else *before* you insist on doing it yourself.
158. When confused, admit it and ask for help.
159. Learn additional skills that can help you on the job. Learn to type, or ten-key by touch, or other computer programs, or welding, or machining, or design work.
160. Look for areas of expertise the company could use, then acquire that knowledge.
161. Accept criticism the same way you accept compliments – with appreciation.
162. Press the reset button on the copy machine before you start making your copies. I'd hate to have to count the number of unnecessary copies I've made by mistake.

163. Be willing to make mistakes. Making mistakes is the 2nd best way to learn.
164. Learn from the mistakes of others. That's the best way to learn, and it'll reduce the number of mistakes you'll make.
165. If a manager is frantic and asks you to do something that's not dangerous or illegal, stop what you're doing and do it without question or hesitation. The manager is frantic for a reason, but wait until later to ask why.
166. Don't spend your break time with someone who's not on a break.
167. Volunteer. Sometimes the worst jobs hide the best opportunities.
168. Do more than is asked of you.
169. Prepare yourself to succeed. Luck happens to people who are prepared. I've read hundreds of stories about people who spent years learning their craft. Then, when an opportunity finally arrived, they were *lucky* enough to become over-night successes.
170. Push yourself. You'll be surprised by what you can accomplish.
171. Meet all deadlines. Don't agree to complete a task by a certain time if you know you can't.
172. If you discover you might miss a deadline, ask for help immediately to get it done.
173. Don't take your job for granted. Remember how much you hate looking for work.
174. Appreciate having your job, and let it show in everything you do. If you don't appreciate having your job, you may not have it very long.
175. If someone asks you a question you can't answer, don't say you don't know – offer to find out and get back to them.
176. Stay focused – concentrate.

177. Take care of yourself. Eat right, get enough rest, exercise, and take vitamins to be healthier and stay more alert.
178. Eat balanced meals and snacks – just like your mother always told you.
179. Limit your caffeine consumption.
180. Minimize your stress at home.
181. Avoid borrowing money – especially on credit cards. The interest rates are outrageous.
182. Separate your home life from your work. When at home, relax, don't act like you do when you're working.
183. Don't overdo it on weekends or vacations.
184. Limit your alcohol consumption 24 hours before work.
185. Don't take illegal drugs.
186. Review your work when you're done. Look at it as if you're the supervisor.
187. Pay attention to the quality of your work. Use a spell checker and double check your math.
188. Don't get overly lost in the details of your job. The big picture is more important.
189. Save 15% of your gross income. You could retire with over a million dollars. This is an investment strategy followed by many self-made millionaires as explained in the book *The Millionaire Next Door*.
190. Keep your head during difficult times. Remember, "This too will pass."
191. Never apologize for being more productive than someone else.
192. Being a good employee is a continuous journey. The moment you think you've arrived, you're no longer there.

5. ORGANIZING YOUR WORK

If you want to be productive, you must be organized.

193. Be at work on time – every day. See *How to Be at Work on Time – Every Day* in Part III.
194. If you don't have a reliable car, use public transportation.
195. Return from lunch 10 minutes early and from breaks 5 minutes early.
196. Empty your bladder before work, at lunch, and during each break. Don't return to your desk just to jump up 15 minutes later and run to the restroom.
197. Don't procrastinate. It never makes a hard job easier.
198. While on the job, put the company's needs ahead of your own.
199. Request any tools or supplies you need to get your work done.
200. Keep your work area neat by putting things away as you go. You'll find that it's easier to locate things when someone else (like your boss) needs them.
201. Plan ahead by mapping out what you need to do each day, each week, and each month – include all deadlines in your plans.
202. Keep a to-do list and a scheduler to remind you of upcoming deadlines, important tasks, appointments, meetings, events, birthdays, and your anniversary. Include long-range projects on your to-do list so you'll know what to do when everything else is done.
203. Never try to remember things. Write them on your to-do list or in your scheduler.

204. Stay on track by reviewing your to-do list each day. It should be the first thing you look at when you arrive, you should refer to it repeatedly throughout the day, and it should be the last thing you look at before you leave.
205. Never eat sloppy or smelly food at your desk or work station.
206. Don't set drinks next to computers or other electronic equipment.
207. Prioritize the items on your to-do list. The following four prioritization categories, and how to use them, are described in the book *Connections: Quadrant II Time Management* by A. Roger Merrill:
    a. Urgent and Important
    b. Important, but not Urgent
    c. Urgent, but Not Important
    d. Not Urgent or Important
208. Always finish your Urgent and Important tasks before you leave for the day.
209. Reward yourself with an enjoyable task after finishing an unpleasant one, assuming all your Urgent and Important tasks are done, and your enjoyable task is part of your job.
210. Store all confidential papers and information in a secure place.
211. Use passwords to protect confidential computer files. Be sure they are passwords you can remember, but nothing obvious like *Password*, your name, address, or phone number.
212. Keep a list of your passwords in a secure place at home – never at work.
213. Do the work now. Save yourself from having to look at it again. If you're reading an email that needs an answer, answer it now. If you don't, you'll have to read it again later. If you do it now, you can move on and forget about it.

214. Don't waste time doing a task better, or more often, than the company needs.
215. When you see a problem, bring it to your supervisor's attention – and always present a recommended solution with it.
216. Get with your supervisor well in advance to schedule vacations and days off.
217. Limit your personal phone calls to 60 seconds or less – no more than three a day.
218. Clean your work area before you leave for the day – your mornings will go much smoother.

6. MEETINGS

Meetings are part of every workplace. They're used to coordinate work within a company and can be the perfect place to showcase your talents, or your stupidity.

219. Try to find out what a meeting is about ahead of time so you can be prepared.
220. Don't be the first or last person to arrive for a meeting. First can be uncomfortable, and last looks bad.
221. Always bring paper and a pen or pencil.
222. Listen to understand, ask questions to clarify, and talk only when requested to do so.
223. Pretend you'll have to teach this same material next time, and take notes if necessary. Your understanding will improve if you do.
224. Concentrate on *what* is right – not *who* is right.
225. Control all bodily emissions.
226. Try to stifle any urge to yawn.
227. If you do yawn, cover your mouth discreetly and yawn quietly – no sighing!
228. Don't be the first or last person to leave – both look bad.

If You're the Speaker

229. Accept your fear. Everyone is afraid of speaking in front of a group.
230. Don't let fear stop you from speaking. Know your subject matter, then channel your fear into an animated presentation.
231. Check all of your buttons and zippers before you enter the room.
232. Don't eat anything sweet before you start. It will dry out your mouth.

233. Don't drink anything carbonated before you speak. Belching isn't the best way to hold an audience's attention.
234. Start and end the meeting on time.
235. Hand out an agenda or outline of what you'll be covering before you begin to speak.
236. Use the handout as your notes and speak from your heart. Never read from a prepared speech, it can be confusing to you and is terribly boring for your audience.
237. Don't imagine your audience naked. It won't relax you.
238. Wipe the corners of your lips if the inside of your mouth feels dry. You don't want that white pasty stuff collecting there.
239. Join a local Toastmasters group. You'll be glad you did.

7. COMPANY FUNCTIONS

Company functions may appear informal, but they aren't. Your actions will be watched closely by both co-workers and management.

240. If possible, attend all company functions, picnics, celebrations, and parties.
241. Maintain a low profile. Be there, but don't try to be the life of the party.
242. Remember, everything you do at a company function will be discussed at length by your fellow employees for many years to come.
243. Even on a warm day, take a jacket to outdoor functions – just in case you need it.
244. Dance with your spouse at least once.
245. Don't discuss work unless someone else brings it up.
246. If offered food, graciously take a little. Don't refuse, and don't be a pig.
247. If the function is in a restaurant, don't order the most expensive item on the menu.
248. Don't be the first person in the buffet line.
249. Avoid messy food, especially spaghetti, anything covered in powdered sugar, or anything that comes with a bib.
250. Take small portions. If you're hungry later, get seconds, but not thirds.
251. If you're at a pot luck, take small portions so you can taste everything. Go back later for more of what tastes especially good.
252. Never bring a fruitcake to a potluck. Does anyone like fruitcake? I suspect fruitcakes take up a large portion of this country's landfills.
253. Brush up on your table manners, and use them.

254. If you're driving, don't drink. Offer to drive others home who have been drinking.
255. If you're not driving, still limit your drinking and stay in control. Drink a tall glass of ice water between each alcoholic beverage.
256. Don't be boisterous.
257. During games, be a good sport. Being competitive is okay, but be willing to lose.
258. Don't crowd your teammates on the volleyball court. Let them hit or miss a few.
259. Avoid playing tug-of-war. Everyone looks stupid pulling on rope, and your body will thank you for not participating.
260. During a softball game, know where the fences are located before you chase a fly ball. I once chased after a foul ball and ran full speed into a chain link fence. Yes, it hurt – a lot.
261. On the golf course, know and obey the rules of the game. When in doubt, add a stroke to your score.
262. Learn the rules of golf etiquette – use them.
263. Don't do anything you wouldn't want photographed and printed in the company newsletter or released onto the Internet.

8. SAFETY

Workplace safety is critical to productivity, company survival, and the health and wellbeing of the staff.

264. If you're sick with something contagious, stay home.
265. Don't run in the office, especially if you're carrying scissors.
266. Lift with your legs, not your back.
267. If something is heavy, don't lift it above your head.
268. Don't pull anything off a high shelf if you don't know how heavy it is.
269. Remove all your personal food items from the company refrigerator at least weekly – and don't eat something if you didn't put it in there.
270. Always lock your car – even if you park in a secured company garage.
271. After dark, don't walk to your car alone if you can avoid it.
272. During lightning storms, avoid high places – like rooftops, scaffolding, or any other place where your body is higher than the surrounding structures.
273. Unplug all electrical equipment during lightning storms.
274. Before you leave the restroom, wash your hands – with soap.
275. If you sit at a desk all day, take a moment every half an hour to stretch your body – a moment, not minutes.
276. If offered a hard hat, wear it.

9. ETHICS & INTEGRITY

Relationships are built on trust. That includes your relationship with yourself.

277. Never promise to do something you can't or won't do.
278. Take pride in everything you do.
279. Don't do anything you can't be proud of.
280. Never compromise your ethics or integrity. If something you're about to do doesn't feel right, you'll respect yourself more if you don't do it.
281. If you don't trust the company's top management, find another job.
282. Politely refuse to do anything you believe is illegal or unethical, even if it is your boss asking you to do it – in which case, consider #281.
283. Be responsible for your actions. If you make a mistake, admit it *before* anyone has to ask you about it.
284. Treat company property better than you treat your own property.
285. Be honest and truthful with yourself and others.
286. Avoid conflicts of interest – these are situations where doing what's right for the company is not in your own best interest. For example, you may wish to buy an old desk that the company doesn't want anymore. If you were the one to set the sales price of the desk, then doing what's right for the company (getting the highest price) isn't in your own best interest (buying the desk for the lowest price). In this case, it would be better for you to ask someone else to set the sales price of the desk.

287. Never borrow anything from the company without permission, even for a little while. It's called *stealing* or *embezzling* even if you're planning to return it.
288. Never lie to your supervisor.
289. Don't do anything sneaky. If you're not sure if it will be okay to make copies of a school project or your personal tax return, ask first.
290. Keep yourself out of personal financial trouble.
291. Never borrow money from a loan shark.
292. Don't seek the approval of other people to strive toward your own goals. Just go for them.
293. Don't seek the approval of other people to do what's right. Just do it.
294. Forgive yourself for your mistakes. Apologize for them, and learn from them, but then move on with your life. Blame, shame, and regret never helped anyone.
295. Be loyal to yourself first. There's nothing wrong with looking for another job. Some companies talk about the importance of employee loyalty, calling anyone who might look for another job as being disloyal. Rubbish. If you look for another job, you'll either find a better job, or you won't. If you do, you'll be happier and more productive. In that case, your family and society will both be better off. If you don't find a better job, you'll know your current job is the best one for you right now, and you're not missing an opportunity. Whether you find a better job or not, you should feel better. What's wrong with that? But never talk about your job search at work. It might upset your co-workers.
296. Find a job that's right for you. The best career opportunity for you may not be the one paying the highest salary.

10. GENERAL

Here are some final assorted secrets and tips for doing well and feeling good at work.

297. Never, under any circumstances, ever utter the words, "I'm bored."
298. Surround yourself with people who have a positive influence on you. In his book *Think & Grow Rich*, Napoleon Hill refers to this as developing a Master Mind group.
299. Avoid people who have a negative influence on you.
300. If you continue to do the same thing, expect to get the same result. If you don't like the results you're getting, change what you're doing or how you're doing it.
301. Know the company's rules and follow them.
302. Let people know you by your productivity – not what you say or how you dress.
303. Check for toilet paper before entering a stall.
304. Unless you're the Public Relations Officer, never talk to the press about the company.
305. Reconcile your personal checking account and credit card accounts every month.
306. Know your command-line. Who is your supervisor, and who is your supervisor's boss?
307. Use your command-line. Always discuss issues with your supervisor first, and avoid going around your supervisor to discuss issues with your supervisor's boss.
308. Don't take instructions from people not in your command-line if those instructions differ from the instructions you've received from the people in your command-line.

309. Be aware of co-workers who seem to have more influence than makes sense for their position. Treat them as if they're managers.
310. If your career isn't progressing as you'd like, or you feel depressed about something, help someone else. You'll both feel better.
311. Learn the basics of supply and demand. It will help you understand the world better. See *Supply and Demand* in Part III.
312. Be patient. Your employer isn't perfect.
313. Don't expect the workplace to be fair.
314. Realize that every problem contains its own solution. If you understand the problem completely, the solution will become obvious. Voltaire said, "No problem can stand the assault of sustained thinking."
315. Every three months, eliminate all caffeine from your diet for two weeks. I read that our bodies build up immunity to caffeine over time. If you eliminate all caffeine from your diet for two weeks, you can reset your body. After no caffeine for two weeks, the kick I've gotten from that first cup of coffee has been amazing.
316. Always get permission before loading personal programs on a company computer.
317. Stay flexible. Interruptions are part of every job.
318. Don't expect praise or additional rewards for doing a good job. A good job is what you were hired to do.
319. When you do receive praise or additional rewards, be gracious and appreciative.
320. Carry paper and a pen or pencil so you can take notes – even if you're not in a meeting.
321. Make sure the company's computer files are backed up regularly and stored off-site. If they aren't, get permission and do it yourself. If there's a fire, you'll be a hero. Nothing is

worse for a company than losing their backup and their computers at the same time. Also, just because a filing cabinet is fire-proof doesn't mean the backup won't melt inside it during a fire.

322. If you're sick, or going to be late, let your supervisor know immediately.
323. Be realistic – some boring and unpleasant tasks are part of every job.
324. If you don't like your job, look for another one. See #295.
325. Never hoard office supplies.
326. Let go of the past. Don't allow anything or anybody to rent space in your head.
327. If you can, buy and use your company's products and services. If available, buy its stock.
328. If you can, buy and use the products and services of your company's customers and vendors.
329. Wear comfortable clothes.
330. If your collar is too tight, wear a bigger shirt.
331. Wear comfortable shoes, even if you have a desk job.
332. Allow yourself to dream of the future, the future you are working toward. Keep those visions clear in your mind. You'll feel happiest whenever you make progress toward your dreams. So, enjoy it when you do make progress. Once you achieve your dreams, dream up new dreams to work toward.
333. Don't let fear stop you. If you know that what you want to do is the right thing for you, then move forward, regardless of your fears.
334. Lead by example. What you say won't be heard over the noise made by what you do.
335. Never lose your sense of humor – or your sense of the ridiculous.

PART III

OTHER IMPORTANT STUFF (OIS)

"Things may come to those who wait, but only the things left by those who hustle."

>Abraham Lincoln
>16th President of the United States

OIS #1 – The 5 Steps to Doing Well and Feeling Good at Work – Worksheet

This worksheet is designed to help you apply the five steps discussed in Part I. If you're unsure of an answer, refer to Part I and discuss it with your supervisor. Try to keep your answers brief and clear. Use a separate sheet of paper to fill in the blanks and answer the questions:

1. The key to my doing well and feeling good is my _____.

2. My company is trying to help the following people _____.

   Do I want to help these people?

   My company helps them by solving the following problems for them _____.

   Do I want to help solve these problems for these people?

   My company's activities contribute to society in the following ways _____.

   Do I want to contribute to society in these ways?

3. My position inside the company is called _____.

   The work I do contributes to the company in the following ways _____.

Do I want to contribute to the company by doing these activities?

4. I am _____ to do whatever I can to help my company.

5. The most important company problem for me to solve is: _____.

Once I've taken care of that problem, the next most important problem for me to solve is:

_____.

I'll try to figure out a way to improve the following activities that I do: _____.

In order for me to be able to solve more problems, the most important skill for me to learn is: _____.

I can learn this skill by doing the following:

_____.

The next most important skill for me to learn is: _____.

I can learn this skill by doing the following:

_____.

OIS #2 – How to Be at Work on Time – Every Day

1. Get the most uninterrupted sleep possible by avoiding the Snooze Alarm – locate your alarm clock out of arm's reach, preferably on the other side of your room. Set it for the time you must get up, no earlier. Sleep straight through until your alarm goes off, then get up. Don't allow yourself to return to bed.
2. Get dressed for work before you eat breakfast – you can always rush out of the house without eating, but you can't rush out of the house without dressing.
3. Keep everything you need to take with you to work together and in the same place – check to make sure they're all there before you sit down to eat your breakfast.
4. Locate a clock in the kitchen where you can see it while you eat – and refer to it often.
5. Don't start reading the news until you're ready to leave the house – consider not reading it at all until after work.
6. Be ready to leave the house at least 15 minutes before you have to leave – these 15 minutes allow you a little leeway for those unexpected preparation delays such as spilling something on your pants or your kids misbehaving.
7. Before you leave home, make sure you have your keys, phone, money, and your glasses.
8. Leave home early enough to arrive at work at least 15 minutes early – 15 minutes allow you enough time to arrive relatively stress free, use the restroom, and get settled so you'll be ready to start work on time. 15 minutes also allow you a little leeway for those unexpected

delays and detours that always seem to happen along the way.
9. Use reliable transportation – whether you drive, walk, ride a bike, take a bus, subway, train, or trolley, make sure the transportation you use will reliably get you to work.
10. If you're driving and running late, don't exceed the speed limit to try to arrive a minute or two sooner – your life, and the lives of those around you, are more important than punctuality, just apologize to your supervisor when you get to work and schedule your time differently tomorrow.

OIS #3 – Handling Difficult Customers

While working as a dining room attendant in a local restaurant some years ago, my son mishandled a difficult customer and got into trouble because of it.

It all started when a customer asked my son where the drink refill was that my son had promised him. My son told the man that he didn't remember promising to get him a refill, and that perhaps he had spoken with someone else. The customer became irate. He was adamant that my son was the one who had promised him the refill and angry that he would deny it.

After spending a few minutes trying to clear up the misunderstanding, my son went and got the man his drink refill. The dining room supervisor pulled my son aside and put him on a two-day suspension for upsetting the customer.

My son was confused. He didn't think he had done anything wrong.

Whenever you're accused of doing something you didn't do, defending yourself is the most natural reaction. Because the customer had accused my son of doing something he hadn't done, he tried to defend himself. He was innocent. But the customer would have none of it. The more my son denied it, the more adamant and irate the customer became.

What did my son do wrong, and how could he have handled the customer better?

The first thing my son had done wrong was to defend himself. So, what's wrong with that? The customer had made a mistake, right? Doesn't matter. No customer is interested in hearing that they made a mistake. What they want is service, not arguments or excuses.

The second thing my son had done wrong was to not apologize. The customer was upset about poor service. He only wanted two things. He wanted someone to say they were sorry, and he wanted someone to get him a refill.

The third thing my son had done wrong was to not solve the customer's problem immediately. The customer was thirsty, and he didn't have anything to drink.

Here are my three rules for handling difficult customers:
1. Never defend yourself or your company.
2. Apologize immediately if you feel there is any misunderstanding.
3. Solve the problem. If you can't, offer to get someone who can.

How could my son have handled the customer better? When the customer accused him of not getting the refill, my son should have said immediately, "I'm sorry. Let me get that for you right away." When he brought the refill, he could have asked, "Is there anything else I can get for you?"

If he had done that, the customer would have calmed down immediately, and my son wouldn't have been suspended.

OIS #4 – Supply and Demand

The easiest way to understand the simple basics of Supply and Demand is to understand what happens when the demand for something changes:
1. If more people want something (Demand), the value of that thing goes up.
2. If fewer people want something, the value of that thing goes down.

People are amazingly inventive. If the value of something goes up high enough because a lot of people want it, someone always figures out a way to provide it for them (Supply).

If the value of something goes down low enough because fewer and fewer people want it, then the people who had been providing it will stop and go do something else.

Supply and Demand affect every aspect of our lives by controlling the problems people try to solve, regardless of their economic, religious, or political affiliation. If enough people want something, someone will figure out a way to get it to them.

Supply and Demand explain why farmers have somehow managed to keep the food supply growing faster than the population. People want food and are willing to pay for it. So, inventive farmers have figured out ways to grow more food on less land.

Supply and Demand explain the persistence of illegal drugs in our society. Regardless of how much money the government spends trying to stop drug trafficking, enough people want drugs, and are willing to pay enough money, that some people are always figuring out ways to supply them.

Supply and Demand explain the growth of big government. Regardless of who's running the country, enough people want the government to protect and care for them that it continues to grow.

It explains the rise of Microsoft. People want their computers more user friendly.

It explains the demise of the buggy whip industry. Fewer people drive buggies. Therefore, they don't need whips.

It explains the drop in typewriter sales. People would rather do word processing on their computers than type on typewriters.

It explains why carbon paper sales have disappeared since 1979. It's easier to photocopy a document after word processing (or just print it again) than it is to type the original with carbon paper.

Supply and Demand motivate people to solve problems.

Understanding the simple basics of Supply and Demand can make the world easier to comprehend and will help ease your fear about the future.

When you hear people talk about impending doom due to over population, food shortages, or whatever, realize that doomsayers have been predicting this since the beginning of mankind.

Regardless of what future problem might come along, someone will always figure out a solution. And that is because the bigger the problem, the more people will be willing to pay someone to solve it.

Supply and Demand, it's a wonderful thing.

OIS #5 – Recommended Reading

1. *No Place To Run* by Tim Shortridge and Michael D. Frounfelter (Vallentine Mitchell, 2002) is an inspirational Holocaust survivor story about David Gilbert, a friend of mine. It is my first published book and the best example of problem solving I've ever seen.
2. *The 7 Habits of Highly Effective People* by Stephen R. Covey (Simon and Schuster, 1989) is one of the most profound books ever written. Dr. Covey provides an insightful analysis of the basic fundamentals for leading a happy and productive life.
3. *Connections: Quadrant II Time Management* by A. Roger Merrill (The Institute for Principle-Centered Leadership, 1987) elaborates on Stephen R. Covey's Habit #3 – Put First Things First and provides additional insights on how to apply it to your life.
4. *The 8th Habit – From Effectiveness to Greatness* by Stephen R. Covey (Simon and Schuster, 2004) is a profound follow-up to Dr. Covey's *7 Habits* book and will help take you to the next level of a purpose-filled life.
5. *Think & Grow Rich* by Napoleon Hill (Fawcett Crest, 1960) is one of the first books (and still one of the best) on how to succeed in life by using your head.
6. *The Millionaire Next Door* by Thomas J. Stanley, Ph.D. & William D. Danko, Ph.D. (Pocket Books, 1996) explains how self-made millionaires accumulate wealth.

OIS #6 – Recommended Learning

Whether you take college courses, check out library books, or read magazine articles, I highly recommend you learn the following:

1. *Business English* – I took a course in junior college and it helped me to communicate better within the corporate environment. Business writing is not the same thing as creative or literary writing, and it helps to know the difference.
2. *Public Speaking* – I attended a Toastmaster's group for two years. It was terrifyingly wonderful.
3. *Basic Accounting* – Knowledge of basic accounting is the best way to understand the financial activity of a business. My book, *Understand Accounting Without Falling Asleep* has helped many of my clients with this subject. I'm mentioning it here because I don't want to list two of my own books under *Recommended Reading,* even though I do recommend all of my books.
4. *Negotiating* – You're negotiating in life far more than you realize. Knowing how to do it better can save you a lot of money. I bought *The Secrets of Power Negotiating* through Nightingale-Conant Corporation's mail-order training ages ago. The book is available on Amazon.
5. *Psychology* – A fascinating subject that I've studied for years. I particularly like the work of Nathaniel Branden. He's written many fine books.

Acknowledgements

This book would not have been possible without the support and assistance of my wife, and best friend, Corky Shortridge. She also happens to be my editor, proof-reader, and best critic. Thank you, thank you, thank you.

Other Books by
Tim Shortridge

Available on Amazon.com

Non-fiction

NO PLACE TO RUN – As told by David Gilbert, written by Tim Shortridge and Michael D. Frounfelter (Vallentine Mitchell, 2002)

David and Sophie Goetzel moved from Germany to Warsaw, Poland in 1937 to escape the rising Nazi anti-Semitism at home. When the Germans invaded two years later, David vowed to keep his loved ones alive.

With dogged determination, the help of people he befriended along the way, and luck, he guided his wife and two-year-old daughter through the siege of Warsaw, imprisonment by the Gestapo, confinement in the Warsaw ghetto, going into hiding on the Aryan side of the city, eventual internment in Bergen-Belsen, and a terrifying train ride that led to liberation in 1945.

David, his wife, and his daughter all survived.

Michael Frounfelter and I wrote this true story about my friend David Gilbert in the style of a suspense / thriller. We've been told it reads as if John Grisham had written ***The Diary of Anne Frank****, but with a happy ending.*

UNDERSTAND ACCOUNTING WITHOUT FALLING ASLEEP: A Simple Explanation of the Basics for Non-Accountants – by Tim Shortridge
(Tim Shortridge, 2015)

Fiction

SEALING FATE – a novel by Tim Shortridge
(Tim Shortridge, 2015)

There's an arsonist on the loose in San Diego County igniting wild fires in the dry, overgrown canyons when–ever the Santa Ana winds blow. Doctor Vanessa Tornen lives with her mother and daughter in a house that over–looks one of those canyons.

When she accepts a position at a women's center, Doctor Tornen thinks she may have finally found the job, and perhaps even the man, of her dreams. Then a group of pro-life fanatics decides to shut down the center by intimidating their employees and their families.

Vanessa's entire world could come crashing down around her, if it doesn't go up in flames first.

OUT OF PLUMB: A Quirky Collection of Humorous Short Stories and Poems – by Tim Shortridge
(Tim Shortridge, 2015)

Need a quick laugh? This humorous collection of quirkiness will have you chuckling in no time.

Made in the USA
Charleston, SC
12 June 2015